About the author:

O.D. Isaac is an author, health care professional, and proud father of two wonderful teenagers, one of whom has autism. "I was inspired to write a book that introduced children to children with disabilities, or as expressed in this book, children who are different. I believe it is critical to teach children at an early age about diversity, acceptance, and appreciation for individuals who may behave differently. A positive perspective of people, and communities, honed in the elementary years can serve greatly in increasing tolerance, respect, decrease in propaganda, and unwarranted perceptions towards those who are different. My goal is that if children can appreciate diversity on the playground, then as adults they will equally appreciate diversity in society at large. Thank you for reading my book, I hope it serves the intended purpose for the reader, and audience as well.

O.D. Isaac

The author's attempt to enlighten the reader about the developmentally disabled in this nature is a fascinating approach. I recommend this book as a must read in our schools as well as in our homes. Understanding and acceptance of children who are different can affect the mindset, interaction and even laws that affect our society. There is no greater investment in educating our youth about co- existing with others who are different be it race, religion, gender and in this case expressive intellect.

Dr. Stanley Goldstein

Hi reader, my name is Bookie, and I'd like to tell you about my friend Willie.

Willie has a hard time speaking, and making friends.

That's why I'm here to talk to you about my good
buddy Willie.

Willie wants you to know that he loves to play basketball, kickball, and soccer, just like you.

And if you give Willie a chance, he would like to play with you.

Some kids on the play ground make fun of Willie because he does not play the same way most kids play.

When Willie sees that he's being teased, he becomes sad, and feels embarrassed. He wishes the cool kids wouldn't tease him.

One day on the playground, brave Brenda saw Willie
being teased, and could see Willie's feelings were hurt.

The very next day, while on the play ground, Willie kicked the ball towards the fence in brave Brenda's direction. Brave Brenda dashed to catch the ball, and kicked it back to Willie with a thumbs up.

"Hi Willie, my name is Brenda, would you mind if we played together". Willie was so excited he quickly kicked the ball back with glee.

Now everyday during recess, brave Brenda plays with Willie on the playground.

Soon, other classmates on the playground joined in playing Willie's favorite game, kickball.

Now Willie has made more friends, and doesn't have to play alone.

Let's hear it for brave Brenda, and the nice kids who play with Willie, even though he is different.

Do you know some one like Willie in your school?

Would you be like brave Brenda, or make fun of them like the not so nice kids on the playground.

Remember, everyone is different, and special in their own way.

We can all play together, and make the playground a great place to have fun.

Willie

Bookie

Brave Brenda

The End.